The Revenant

first edition

Rev. C

I0150096

Joseph Leo Hickey

&

Amelia Vandergast

www.MelodiumHouse.com

joseph@melodiumhouse.com

Part 1: Absence

"To be so lovely and so lost. To be all answerful with all that knowing trapped inside. To be beautiful and broken."

— Patrick Rothfuss, *The Wise Man's Fear*

mortality

as we processed
the passing years,
we feigned
knowledge of the things
we had lost
as we walked
on the endless fields of
grass, the light
dropped into our hearts
we thought
we knew the meaning of songs
but we no longer remembered
dancing or energy or the motion of it
you were destroyed without mercy
age marched on
and took what we thought
we never
would have a chance to hold
so close to our hearts
that its spirit
would burn through us like lava
that the devils
that haunted our footsteps
would crawl into our dreams
and we would never let anyone
know what we were dreaming about

lust

our lust grew inside us
and
the wind was howling down
the street
with a scent that would cover
the world
and a voice it had forgotten,
and the same voice rose out
of the shadows
and spoke,
and then she appeared
walking silently through
the abyss,
warming her hands
that had not touched another
in a couple of decades

truth that would draw
us together in love

Serenity walked
through
the empty
streets where
the echoes
of
voices long gone
return in her voice,

she walked past
        the empty forest,
where she dreamed of growing closer
to the memories she would never possess again

the world followed her

as she walked,
the world followed her
as she found
herself still unwelcomed
by a world that had rejected her,
a world that she had fallen into

and words
had been forgotten,
been lost in the uncertain oceans
of trepidation

she walked so far
she had almost left the city,
she had become bonded with her fears
and they walked beside her,
she remembered flashes of light
and
sharp objects cutting her side open,
she remembered the mind is
easily open
when you let yourself be
taken over by the forces
of truth that invade
the spaces where you always thought
you were comfortable,
and the oceans tempted her
to come and dive into their abyss
she became close friends
with those who
never met her,
she began to live life
as if she had never died
and tried to find herself
in the empty space between
charity and denial,
life and desertion,
desperation
and truth,

her father wept over her body
        and then gambled what was left
of his money,
and learned to
fire a pistol,
and learned
to steal to survive

and Serenity waited outside the
prison,
where her father sat and wept,
but he didn't recognize her,
he only watched as she asked him a thousand questions
but was led out of the room
before she could ask them all

and then she left the prison
and went to her mother's grave
and laid a flower on the grave
and then the flower wilted
and blew across the city because of the breeze
and then pop stars took the flowers
that had wilted
and played music as the flower bounced
off their guitars,
the wilted flower flew across
to another city,
where trash littered the streets
this rose ended up in a trash can
and it was incinerated with the rest
of the trash,
and burned so much that its chemical
makeup was destroyed
and when the chemicals
were finally gone,
these chemicals flew up into space
and reached the moon,
where the gods of ancient Greece
waited patiently for
the last believer to reject them

and Serenity walked the path to the homeless shelter
and applied for a job
as a trash person to clean up the city
that was overflowing with trash,
they didn't accept her for the position
so she went and did it for free
and stood outside as people watched
and the whole world followed her
as she began to sing
a song she had only known
before the first time she died,
and she was the only one alive
who had been dead before,
she was the only one in the world
that had seen the other side,
then one day she decided to tell people
who she was and that
she was really
Serenity come back to life
but since
no one could document where she
came from, they sent her to an asylum
where she waited for a year or so
for the time on the wall to expire,
and she spilled all her truth
about the monster that ended her life
and the memory of the sad lament
and kiss of Pain
and she thrived in the nights
when there was no one moving
at the corner of the ward,
            and she admired the sunlight
in the mornings and fell deeply
and madly in love with this sunlight
            and then
they led her out of the ward
and threw her violently onto the street
where the same cycle repeated again
and again
the same days she spent alone,

she knew she had changed so much
but the world had not changed at all,

recovery

she vanished into the crowd
of a million lonely people,
she vanished into the chasms
where there is no emotion
in the hearts of men and women,
she walked with you as you labored
and then lay next to you as you went to bed and fell asleep,
absolutely alone,

she walked back to her high school
and saw that it had been abandoned,
no students would ever walk there again,
she felt inebriated with
toxic feelings that nothing was happening
the innocence lost
the death
of feelings that consume the soul,
the waiting and then the falling,
into the river
and floating through the river

the tragic embrace of poetry

hope returns

she held a candle and walked with you
leading you out of a nightmare

memory

she remembered the warmth and the smiles
in the summer,
as her back was against the concrete wall of the building
her long black hair covering her face,

union

she grew closer to those
who she thought she would never understand
when she slipped down through
into ambiguity,

you dreamed of things
that had no fulfillment
and no payoff,
but you knew you wanted
to become successful at achieving those dreams

mockery

we do not have time in the world to sit idly by
while the scoffers
roar

there is always music

you know that our songs
which we sang in the darkness
drown out the songs you
sing in the light of day
to stadiums of people

Part 2: Resurgence

"What is wanted *(by religion)* are blindness and intoxication and an eternal song over the waves in which reason has drowned."

— Friedrich Nietzsche, Daybreak: Thoughts on the Prejudices of Morality

resume game

do you want to know
what happens after death?
does the fragility

of your mortality quiver at the thought?

you're right to tremble

perhaps it's best that life prepares you for the onslaught

the reprieve
which you've so desperately
sought is the greatest lie ever told

tune in tune out

think of death
as a windowless room
with a TV screen as the only source of light
you tune in,
and watch
the ones you love wither and rot
in their mortal form as they tear themselves apart over the
inconsequential,
the banal, and the inane
you get to see the shackles of capitalism, communism, false
religion, fascism, extremism in all of its forms,

 narcissism

in all of their chastising glory

the oppression is always so well justified,

but if only it ended with justification
and didn't transcend into elation

for people to rise,

others need to fall,

balances of power perpetually transpose

until there's nothing left to lose,
and the unlucky
get to join me,
and all of
the other host-less souls
in a room with a view
to our worst nightmares unfolding;
being forgotten and replaced
when i got to walk amongst the living,
each footstep was taken in a blind direction,
frantically hoping
that it would lead to validation,
a feeling of safety,

a feeling
that i truly had a place in the world,

that i would mean something to someone
for a time,
people still returned to my poetry,
finding comfort

in my comfortless words born of nihilism and contempt,
but that soon ended,
they regarded me
as a hero for a time,
but it wasn't long
until i was only briefly
remembered on the day i died,
and the day i was born,

as though nothing of great consequence happened in between

reanimation

Hollywood. lied again
it didn't happen
as they usually portray
there was no sharp intake of breath
no instant shock snap back into animation
i felt my heartbeat first
slowly pumping
cold blood around my body,
sating my organs as they started to pulsate
the rhythm of my mortal coil resumed
sure, i felt a little hollow,
but what's new?

shout out to my killer

in a way, i was grateful
that my death
wasn't tinged with my own despair,
~~can anyone really say~~
~~that they've never thought about ending it all?~~
~~placing the gun in their own hands~~
~~and pulling the trigger of solace?~~
the world never existed for me anyway,
poets, artists, cinematography, it could all distract me,
but it was a constant struggle to feed blips of bliss into my mind
most people wore masks,
but in mine i suffocated
it had no opening for a mouth,
i had no words
left to speak in the end,
every exchange
left me feeling short changed
in the end i was in debt,
with nothing left to give

to me or anyone around me
in my time in stasis,
i realized,
people can be
as much of a plague to others,
as they are the earth
land is raped for oil,
women raped for dominance
forests are cut down
people are torn apart
it's the survival of the fittest
i always knew i wouldn't last long
i could
never picture myself growing old
it wasn't that i didn't believe in happy endings

i just knew,
my life wouldn't work that way

a banal new world

through my ethereal keyhole
to the world,
i could only see
what i knew to be real
in living form

i could revisit people and places,
but never see
outside of the closed periphery
which
i came to believe was everything

now i've been given
the chance to live again,
not defined by what i had done before,
i have no obligations to the living

not anymore

i no longer have to fit in,
because i don't have a place,
there are no tables with spots reserved for me,
there's no one i can disappoint by hiding away
and pulling back the veil of the true nature of humanity by
reading *1984* and realizing that the
the resistance fighters are
never going to win their war,
the machines will always spit on those who live and die poor

bubble obliteration

my biggest questions
lay outside of my own existence

now, i see it

for how odiously small it was

the smallest things always mattered when there were eyes
to see my idiosyncrasy
were my clothes in poor taste?
did pity rise up in
their throats as they saw me presenting myself into the world
awkwardly?
or did i force that own bitter pill down my throat?
what did they think of me after my admittances that i never liked
Green Day or Blink-182?

did they realize my boredom
of every routine within the world
had reached the highest pinnacle

did they talk behind my back about the excessive number of
Instagram pics in which i faked a smile
despite living in a broken world?
did i want to reconnect with the past, when it did
so little to make me want to stay?
i lay
with dampened pillows so many nights
my cheeks started to feel raw,
but i could do little to prevent the hate and love which would
pour from me
i see no reason to go back there
where humiliation
and degradation were rife
and the artillery which
abstracted me was the deftest touch i had felt in years

lost in fiction

i could only turn to fiction for answers

but i found myself

with even more questions

could i draw parables
between myself and The King of the North?
there was no Lord of Light
to thank for my resurgence
no great mission lay in front of me,
but there was air in my lungs,
the New York sky line in my periphery,
and the hum of humanity in my ears,
and that was enough for me

my first acquaintance

a splintering park bench
lay under an apple tree
just on the outskirts of town
it looked as good a place
as any to acclimatize to my freshly renewed mortality
sunlight was breaking
through the city smog,
it gently warmed my skin,
reminding me
just how beautiful it is to feel alive,
the smallest sensations;
wind breezing through your hair,
hearing the innocence of birdsong,
feeling grass beneath your feet
i breathed through gratitude for the first time in my life,
feeling my lungs swell with actualization;
a completeness, unburdened with the demand for anything but
this perfect moment

a bottle of wine remained
from the previous occupant
i started to remember
how it felt
to drink and to forget
many bottles had lain beside me
some sweet
some sour
but never more bitter than what already lingered inside of me

death felt a relief
but now, the reprieve i once so desperately sought
had been stripped away and
the stage light
shined upon me once more
but there are no demands
that i don a painted guise
and contort my replies
so they meet expectation

i hadn't spoken at all in 25 years

i forgot the force of will it takes to force vibrations
out of your throat in perfect sequence
the hum reverberated through me,
it took all of my energy
not to burst out into song
i still remembered
all my favorite lyrics

i carried the words
of resonance to the afterlife,
it was only then i realized
the true value in music
souls exposed,
emotions candidly raw;
an invitation to true human experience,
a life line,
a connection
that not even death can cut
as i uttered words under my breath
hoping they'd find the right arrangement and wouldn't stumble
i was too distracted to notice the proximity of the children
playing soccer on
the field just in front of me

i was sure they wouldn't be able to hear me,
but i got my first taste of humiliation
the lurching sickness was just as transposing as before
i wished for
the ground to swallow me whole
knowing
it would only spit me back out again
i stood to leave
only to feel a hand on my shoulder
my skin prickled with the heat,
i wanted to kiss the stranger to feel a flood of the same warmth,
but i was aware of how out of place i looked,

and how out of this world i would be

i was ashen, weary, frantic,
he was poised, polished, refined, slicked back blonde hair,
perfectly angular dominant features

there was the sense that for his whole life everything fell into his
lap – especially women

but somehow, his eyes melted into mine, offering a
serendipitous synergy,
only for him to ask me the time

i looked at the sky and suggested it to be around midday,
i wondered where he needed to be while hoping he would never
leave but the moment was as fleeting as any in this world
frustration and impatience furled across his brow
the clock was ticking,
it's always ticking,
down,
down,
and further down -
never higher,
time never allows you to transcend
after he took a few paces away from me
he turned on his heel
and as though it was an afterthought
asked for my number,
as though the distance permitted him bravery, and rejection
was easier to swallow a stone's throw away
he didn't believe me that i didn't have a phone
i couldn't quite believe it either
for years of my life, i stared into that black mirror
urging it to permit me happiness,
allowing me to believe that happiness
was only in reach when my phone was
he made his way back towards me,
holding a wad of cash and his business card
"if you want to be connected to the real world,
find a way to call me"
i watched his silhouette
disappear into the city in the direction of the skyscrapers
trying to place the emotion
coursing through me,
but it felt alien
was it by chance that the kindest exchange of my life
came from a stranger when there was no expectation?

the years i spent yearning for affection

suddenly seemed even more bitter

a procrastinating world

i left a world which was desperate for change
turning to the nihilism of Nietzsche,
and the existentialism of Sartre for their philosophy,
unable to take the stagnation
trying to bring art into fruition to dilute the torment
while worshipping monochrome portraits
i found handfuls of them to bow to
all the while knowing
that they also knew what Wilde said to be true
"it is the ugly and the stupid who have it best in this world"
stupidity was a privilege i was never granted
it was something i actively discarded,
unaware of how it had shielded me
from the loss of hope which came to define me
humanity felt like an exposed nerve twitching in malicious
rhythm
as for my aesthetic,
my face was a painted target,
my fashion sense a fetish
i kohled my eyes
dressed in studded leather,
it was my uniform,
my attempt to warn the world
of my intensity
whether it was love or hate,
everything had to be felt viscerally

life had to feel like i was grasping
a lemon squeezing every drop of pleasure and torture
until my muscles
 knew the same ache which lingered in my heart

who stopped the clock?

i see nothing new
there's a coffee shop on every corner
frequented by suited men with furrowed brows
fueling their half-lives consumed
possessed by materialistic desire

just as many poor line the streets,
if not more
tattered clothes
begging for change
they get coins thrown at them instead
the gutters still offer a putrid aroma,
and garbage bags line the streets,
the sounds on the streets are the same

there's a cacophony of frustration
it almost sounds harmonious,
i can see the beauty in the chaos now,

how bored would we be if the world always went our way?
we can't rely on change to be our salvation
the same songs are still played on the radio
R.E.M.
The Beatles
Bowie
they're all still here
reminding me that it was like i never felt,
i let the melodies resonate,
the choruses catch,
the rhythm arrest my own pulses,
but it may as well have been to birdsong
or sirens on their way to tend to tragedy
the concordance which

used to speak to my soul just wasn't the same
i stopped asking for something from the music,
instead, i simply allowed to it for what it was

i was no longer looking to be saved
my mind is one with the world again,
but i was under no illusion my soul is owned,
bargained,
butchered,
that was the compromise
which saw my return
i was merely a pawn in a bigger game. i never saw the dice being
rolled, but i had to navigate the snakes and ladders all the same

dinner for one

my entire existence had been trapped in alienation
loneliness crept in to check on me every hour;
it was my most reliable visitor
it was always on time to ensure that i remembered the crushing
weight of my failure
in love. not just romantic love, to which we're all so transfixed,
what i really envied was for someone to love me,
without wanting to fuck me,
without wanting some salacious payoff

i never made any admission,
i only felt the shame
of my burden on the world
i pleaded,
night after night
to feel complete
only to lay down in ennui-laden defeat,
hoping to feel someone who would relish in the task of wiping
the tears away from my cheek
before uttering words which granted resolve
and affirmed what the quotes said to be true
"it's okay not to be okay",
but they only
ever existed on the screen and that person never came,
i never even knew their name,
but i came to the love that stranger
like it was my closest confidant;
they knew it all
my construction operated phantasm
was malleable to my demands,
responsive to my contrition
is there any chance of finding you now,
now that i have an even bigger secret
to lurk over me and blister my memories?
is resurrection a red flag?

love/hate

it took me coming out of the dark to realize
that it was never life i hated

how could i find complaint at the array of colors
the sky would effervescently shine
when the sun set?
how could i hate those fractures of serendipity
which always let me know
greater forces were at work?
how could i forget the rush of adrenaline
reading Plath, Dylan, and Thomas?

no, it was never life that i hated
it was people
and their commodified exchanges
where anything could be currency;
empathy,
love,
support,
acclaim,
comfort,
everything is for sale
yet,
there's no value left in the world,
at least there never was for me
i felt the boot prints
from those who would walk all over me, leaving the demand to
smile in braille on my skin
because self-pity was a grotesque sin,
indulgence was frowned upon –
no matter how far down you've been driven into the ground

how far did you go?

25 years later,
i knew just where to find her
it feels as though i've only just left her
time doesn't pass
when time doesn't exist
mortality is a flame
which death puts out
i'm unsure of why i sought her out
but i remembered the way
she always used to see me
as if she was seeing a kaleidoscope of color
she never spoke to me,
but i figured it would be easier to make acquaintance with a
stranger
i found her,
as wide-eyed as ever
maybe that was just her response
when she clapped eyes on me
and screamed my name;
i'd almost forgotten it

she asked for nothing but my embrace
she stroked my limp hair
until i felt inclined to fall into her completely
when she pulled away and gazed at the despondence in my eyes
i knew at this point i should cry,
but emotions are hard to find
when you've had none to feel for 25 years
i've transcended self-pity
gifted with the knowledge
that we're all just accidents of consciousness,
over-cooked chimps with anxiety
overcomplicating the world with new labels
and justifications
i almost started to miss the knots of anxiety;

the only companion who would ever really know me
and show me that it cared by allowing my throat to close around
vowels,
and turn a static world into a carousel-
there'd be no telling how long it would take to ride it out

but here i am
in her living room,
green tea in hand
as i hear her daughter
play crass records from her room,
looking at the lines she'd collected on her face,
somehow it made me wish that i'd collected some too,
but for 25 years my body was untainted,
while my soul grew wiser with each passing second

she found out that i was pregnant
on the day i died

i saw the family portraits hanging on the wall
no sign of a father,
just the two of them,
bonded by their joint abandonment
she eventually asked me the questions
i hoped i wouldn't have to hear

the how's, the why's, i didn't have an answer for
after the disappointment of my confusion
it was hard to discuss the new developments in town,
but my attention piqued at the mention of a new record store
'Serenity records'
there's only one person i knew who would preserve my memory
hawking pieces of plastic

a cry for war is a cry for death

restlessness became a constant twitch,
forcing me from place to place,
with every new destination
i felt the disappointment
through lack of epiphany
that 'this is exactly where i need to be'
i found myself in a bar,
whiskey sour in hand,
savoring each drop as the bitter nectar warmed me
in the corner, the TV screen screeched with fear,
the same fear that's been played on repeat for centuries,
the handfuls of people did their best to ignore it,
after all, they came here to forget
but who could ever forget the face of the politicians who pulled
the strings so tightly it was almost like having a noose around
your neck?
news headlines flashed across the screen

"our Enemies ready to strike"

"emergency summit meeting to discuss the possibility of a nuclear fallout"

"get out of the city while you still can"
"millions predicted to die this coming Tuesday"

the announcements
were interrupted by your usual infomercials selling
antidepressants, holidays in the sun, fake tan, probiotic yogurts
the normality almost seemed macabre
around the threats of death
but how else would we spend our last days?

if only the real Viking armies had been televised,
would we see the glamor amongst the gore?

52

crossed swords and splintered shields seem almost romantic
compared to hydrogen bombs
elements of nature weaponized
just as ore had been turned into bludgeoning axes
perhaps there is no better example of humanity;
we create and destroy in equal measure
ensuring that we don't just leave a trace
we leave anguish and blood in our wake
maybe if more people saw the other side,
they'd be less inclined to put others there
and more inclined to make declarations of love
knowing that those three words would keep the departed warm
when you don't even get to feel the temperature
everything you take for granted
is another thing you will miss when the lights go out

standing in the flames

he said "i'd like to see
your foolishness end
with a few sticks and a torch"

i didn't walk away this time
i strode amongst them,
batting their "convert or burn" placards from my face
as they foamed with falsified virtue

weather-beaten and vandalized
"where is your Pope?" i teased
knowing what they always feared;
their religion is a lie

they chanted, blood pressure elevated

"a new savior is amongst us
more of the dead walk amongst the living than you realize
and only a few of us walk on the side of the light"

"whore"

"is that what God would say?"

flashback

i dug my nails into my skin
hoping to feel anything
outside of my mind

with blood drawn
and skin subtly lacerated,
i felt put together,
i felt no reason to be afflicted by the weather
and its desire for me to be happy

as the sun shone with a mocking gaze
the blades of grass became tendrils of torment
love songs on the radio
reminded me how shallow desire could be,
but it was a constant reminder that the world
didn't have to be so cruel
i tapped my pen to the melody
hoping words would fall from me
but all i felt was the static
of isolation coursing through me
how could i be a poet,
if i never wrapped my soul around another's?

i tried painting what reminded me
of the unequivocal truth
telling myself that one day,
someone would want to take my hand
and lead it through the rain
there'd be cyclones of passion
kicking up lust
as it furls its angry teeth around us
perhaps i'd watched *High-Fidelity*,
one too many times
dreaming of a weary soul
who i had the power to complete
but all i see are the caveats
red flags instead of red roses,
not that i'm the romantic type,
but for the most part,
i have no control
in the direction in which my mind flows
no dam could stop it,
i feel the emotion swell over the embankments
then i remembered
my romantic expectations
could only be sated
with metaphysical fashion

and the constructions of love
which had warmed me
night after night
were fires never destined to be lit
i held the matches
in the most merciless of downpours
hoping,
praying for ignition
only to feel my own passion dissolve

end scene

my death came back to me before the rest of my life
 i remembered how the impact of each bullet,
even though the scars had somehow been erased

the sweet rip of bliss tore through my skull
the skull that i had loved and known
but as the blood poured
i couldn't help but feel,

i'd like to spend a little more time within it,
listen to my favorite record; just one more time
look at his photograph; just one more time
feel the waves break over my feet; just one more time
experience the rush of adrenaline as i finish a poem;
just one more time
have an orgasm;
just one more time
drink a beer just one more time
those things never helped me to hold on before
they were small comforts in a world which

my body seemed to react to with visceral contempt
my last breaths were choked with confusion,
but i knew i had to save face in front of the shooter

no one else stuck around to witness my slaughter
there was no inch of remorse on his face
once the bullets left me perforated
i thought i'd seen anger before,
but his face contorted before my eyes
in a way which made me believe that demons existed,
i figured i would find out pretty soon,
that's when my thoughts turned to you
and the words i would choke out
if blood wasn't pouring from between the lips you left un-kissed
if my diary could see me,
it would think me a hypocrite
i had told it night after night in eloquent prosaic ways
my heart had an arrow through it
in love with the idea of being alive
i couldn't bring myself to resign to the fear
in an ugly battle with mortality –

wide eyed grotesque panic
flailing as organs fail
through jagged breaths i savored
the intensity of the daylight
i drank in for the last time
until my nihilistic bubble popped
and i couldn't help but smile,
knowing that this was the end
and this end doesn't have a start
there was no time for unanswered questions,
only abstraction from the anxiety;
my lips curled
in the way i thought my toes would between the bedsheets
belonging to the man i loved -
red was always my color

radical compassion

we push away trauma,
and embrace the torture it offers
there's a humility in caressing your scars and confronting the
proverbial blade
one which many aren't strong enough to swallow
it was my greatest regret through my time in stasis,
allowing someone else to be the architect of my mind,
chiseling shame and lament into me
i imagined his eyes
when he saw me
a sublime cocktail of terror and guilt
would it please me,
as much as it pleased him to put fear in my eyes?
will i drink in the agony
and intoxicate myself with a great thirst?

arriving at the door of his family home i knocked,
as my fist pounded the wood
my mind flooded with regret
why am i not holding a blade?
why did i come here underprepared?
my fingernails dug into my palm
as i listened to fumbling in the hallway,
was he drunk again,
just as he was that night?

as the bolt was drawn back
those black eyes were the last thing i wanted to see
but they weren't there
only clouded blue orbs stared past me
way into the yard
but my voice spoiled the surprise
"Serenity, is that you?"
"you know i died"
"and now i can feel that you're alive"

there was no apology,

but none was needed
after i realized it was me with the power to make the shame and
hurt dissipate all along
this wretched creature who
i prayed would die could not grant me absolution

in the expanse of the darkness
all i wanted was for this moment to come
for it wasn't the man who shot me dead
whose blood i wanted to taste
it was him
i'd repressed it

for so long
only when the life poured out of me,
i could truly see
whose insidious touch
scarred me the greatest
in a time when my innocence
hindered me
i was a child;
much to his delight
two wrongs don't make a right,
but here i stand,
no weapon in hand,
but he never needed one
he just possessed his own body,
and that was enough to make me want to leave my own
it had belonged to him from that point on
now, it belongs to no one
i didn't have to take his eyes,
to leave him blind
that misfortune happened upon him without my intervention
i swallowed the temptation to ask questions of how it happened,
but i've already come to understand
that the universe's will is never underhand

i walked away
knowing that karma was never the bitch we all said she was
she was loyally compassionate

clock hands

i found myself outside Grand Central Station
watching swathes of people scurry along
under the pretense that they are above
the creatures branded as vermin
but perhaps rats have the awareness that they have a tail between
their legs
maybe rats are above the grandiosity;
sewers are no place for mediocrity
maybe they have no awareness of the construct of time;
a clockwork system which commands obedience
sun dials,
hourglasses,
iPhones,
they all remind you that time is running out
people live,
as though the clock hands won't break,
the mechanics won't fail
what happens if you're like me,
and you have to face the consequence of your bin being
unemptied
as you fall to the floor?
my torn out diary pages lay there
scribing through my hysteria
my pen lay against the page so hard
the paper started to tear
through the weight of my ink-dripping blunted sword
perhaps it's true what they say,
it is mightier,
but using it as my only means of resolution weakened me
i could never be the girl to instigate confrontation,
instead,
i'd shy away,
find less reasons
to make people want to leave

but in the end i always stood alone and only my diary knew how the poison of modernity ruined me

i wondered whose eyes gazed upon the words which were all supposed to be left unread

did they have new compassion once they heard of my death?
i think of the floods of crocodile tears shed in my name
the lies made up now i wasn't around to contest them
or did they talk of my self-destruction?

how i loved to test my limits just to feel some semblance of
emotion outside of depression

an explanation

i suppose you're wondering how i returned,
truth is that i never left
no one who has ever died truly ever does
you'd think the world would be overly crowded,
you'd think that the living wouldn't be able to move for the
bones of ghosts,
but space is yet another construct,
just as we all followed the demands of time,
we became limitable by the concept of space
it kept us rooted,
grounded,
afraid
we so eagerly ingested the fear,
we gorged upon it,
while simultaneously finding a way to amplify other's fears
domestic abuse,
systematic governmental oppression,
media sensationalism,
Stanley Kubrick,

it's likely that no one has ever lived and died
without force feeding fear
in exchange for power;
a validation of significance
in a world defined by inconsequence
we're all so eager to make our marks,
but so few of us truly do,
Shakespeare,
Mozart,
Einstein,
one day,
their names will also inevitably fade

people constantly talk about keeping memories alive,
but what if memories never truly die?

people are always too afraid to believe
that the afterlife is beyond their comprehension
a ceased existence,
heaven and hell,
reincarnation,
everyone is always so sure in what they believe,
so assured that there is nothing left to understand
we may be able to get to the moon,
but in reality,
we're like ants trying to understand an iPhone
the afterlife is closer than you think
the veil between the living and the dead is paper thin,
think of it as the difference between turning a light on and off,
there's a serenity in the dark,
every obligation
every need
every greed
every fantasy
is stripped away and replaced by static
you'd never ask for anything but white noise
from a radio wave no longer in use,
that's essentially all we are
frequencies with appetite,
our bodies aren't what we believe them to be
we can look into mirrors
and only see what our eyes project
we can see death,
as the end of life,
or we can see it for what it truly is,
a freedom,
but you're half right
with the concept of hell,
after our bodies fail us
we're powerless to what we see,

the corruption,
the oppression,
the world cannot sustain us anymore
war doesn't just impact the living
but also the dead
we're forced to watch,
or see nothing at all,
how long can you sit in a darkened room before your sanity
starts to fray?
so, why am i here?
call it a martyr's privilege
penance was granted,
and for the first time,
i'm valuable left alive

incanted

someone once told me that we can reinvent ourselves every day

when we wake up,

we choose what kind of person we're going to be,

but as incantations of our own truth,

we see that there's everything to lose in change

a sea of possibility rarely tempts us away from the shallow pool
of familiarity where we know our feet will always touch the
ground, and our heads will always be above water
so, we adopt our most likeable personas
and parade them with the hope of gaining personability points
then wonder why we feel so disjointed

would he welcome me back
if i showed them the true face of resurrection,
or will 25 years have erased every trace of affection?
would he protest to me knowing more than he does?

he always liked the intellectual superiority
which placed him in the power seat

questions shot through my mind like poisoned darts
permitting me to wonder if there was something in the air which
bound my lungs until they were too compressed
to function in natural rhythm

part of me felt a burden,
but not after i saw his face,
i knew exactly where he'd be.
to him, i'm a memory,
but to me, he's the one i followed fondly
in my absence,

i saw Pain privately mourn for me,

he always told me he was incapable of feeling emotion

i never believed him,

visceral stabbing torture tore through him,

 i could always see it in his eyes

on his darker days his eyes

would follow suit, there was no light to be found in them,

just a dark inviting depth which made

you want to find a way to illuminate them

i knew deep down, that our misery was the same,

but back then, i was foolish enough to believe that anyone was

capable of offering a resolve
in my years without a pulse,
in my years of phantasm paralysis
it finally sank in,
abstraction is simply a distraction,
comfort, has to come from within
going on vacation,

may as well be shooting up heroin,

we're all looking for an escape,

we're all looking for ways to dilute the rage once the façade has
been torn off and

the nature of true humanity has been exposed

still, i wanted to offer my own shoulder to cry on,

 perhaps for my own pleasure

i'd always relished in comforting others for personal
gratification,
in the end i gave my life for it,
ultimately, i knew,
the people who surrounded me

as shots were fired had a better chance of happiness
it's been a while since i've seen him cry,
he'd pulled himself out of the dark without my hand

part of me wished that seeing my face would allow the ketchup
bottle to burst so i have a reason to hold him,

pushing all rationality aside
part of me resented myself for wanting

my life to be validated by tears

i recounted the final poem ever written for him

"debauchery and dreamscapes

you've already slipped between my thighs a thousand times in my mind
you fed me the frustration; forced it into me
scratched me until i bled and constricted each breath
until the next felt meaningless

you let me carve my name between the synapses of your intellect
you let them snap, fire, and relay the neural itch
as we both felt the sanctity of my subjugation
you let me use my power as a sacrifice
allowing your sanctity to taste that a little bit sweeter
i've already craved you until i was sure i knew the taste
i've already felt the weight of your heavy hands
as they led me to absolution
taking the leeches off my chest
never laying to rest what lingers between us;
the phosphorous fire
which will burn
until i find an outlet for the adoration
which is only open in your arms"

i'd repressed the urge to send it to him countless times knowing
the rejection which would follow would leave me feeling more
ashamed than ever

that i'd surrendered my heart to someone
who always thought they could do better

shuttered Oasis

i'd found myself amongst the most run down streets in Brooklyn
they used to be a bohemian Oasis,
street performers used to stand on every corner, 8 foot angels,
mime artists,
buskers with their renditions of Tom Waits, Leonard Cohen,
Nick Cave... all of the aural alchemy poured through disheveled
guitars and dirt-stained hands
rapturous laughter used to echo from the coffee shops,
frequented by bands of art degree toting liberals all coming
together in the name of expression and progression
you could taste the virtue in the air
but now, shutters had slammed down for the final time long ago
on most of the stores,
lone figures skulked along the dimly-lit streets,
propaganda was plastered on every surface,
burnt out stores were now hateful message boards, spreading the
angst that there was no other outlet for
two shops on the expansively grey street remained open
a record store, and a liquor store;
everything you could possibly need to numb the torment
i had no desire to ingest the bitterly numbing elixir, or to find my
place in the world by possessing a piece of cultured plastic
i just wanted to see him
sitting behind the desk of the record store
he had the window lined up with the classics from Joy Division,
Killing Joke, and The Cure
"got anything by the Pixies?" i asked,

he was half way through detailing his collection of rare singles,
limited edition presses imported from the UK
when he truly saw me
"i thought i'd drop by i haven't seen you in a while"
we smoked a few joints in silence,
i waited for the twitch in his left eye to calm
it was always his idiosyncrasies that endeared me to him, little

charisma to speak of, but he was a frenzy of complexity which
tore me away from the monotony of what it was to be human
i must have looked a child to him now
he was in his 40s, with a hairline which slightly receded and a
stomach which protruded more than it used to
his eyes seemed duller – they had lost their hunger, lost their
fight
pity dared to swell in my chest,
i swallowed it down in the refusal to let time pour sorrow over
this moment

i may have been resurrected for five days before i got the nerve
to speak to him,
but it was precisely the moment where he told me

that he loved me i truly felt alive

if only he didn't follow up with the words
"back then, when we were kids"

i guess Morrissey was wrong, all lights do go out
across his face was a more pressing concern than my
manifestation in his world

his hands trembled, his eyes appeared sore,

even though we'd sat for hours without a single tear falling

"i think this is the end, Serenity" he muttered with a whiskey
glass pressed to his still to this day delicate lips

it was almost like nothing had changed but the degree of
certainty that the Armageddon we'd been waiting for

was finally on our door step

it didn't matter who opened the door,
we all had to accept the call from terror

Part 3: Purpose

*"I sat in the dark and thought:
There's no big apocalypse. Just an
endless procession of little ones."*
Neil Gaiman

the joy in the nightmare

tear us from the lie
that reality is taintless
or unmolested,
let the facades of culture
which have glossed over the rot decay too,
set the maggots free to tremulously writhe

don't tend to your scars,
let them ooze, weep and stain,
there's no time left for divinity,
we are putridity in infected form

whether it's the ashen bones of sinners
or the flesh of virginal virtue
everything erodes,
nothing remains
and so it must be,
for the world to have a chance at purity

be gratified for every nightmare
every single
screaming
searing cinematic portrayal of frustrative fear
where you're powerless
motionless to the horror
directed by your own mind
lynchian Mise-En-Scenes
are your salvation from naivety

your ghosts are redemptive forces,
urging you to grow
you should have learned to trust them
while you were still alive,
they never had any reason to fail you,
unlike the living
the living never forewarned you

about the oncoming paradigmatic shift
only blinded you with fairy tales
making you believe that happy-ever-afters weren't just fiction
in a world of safety
embrace the dark,
find the visceral meaning,
don't let beauty distract you

let your complacency shatter,
offer it to brutal hands to tear apart,
subject yourself to the subversions of the truth,
your eyelids being prized from comfort is always going to hurt

sufferance stifled is a life wasted
kick through the paralysis,
make love to toxic lust

embrace the surrealist's wisdom

youth paradox

my body hasn't aged a day,
but there's an ache in my bones;
a dull anguish which i never experienced in my 'youth'
i wince through it,
clutching the knowledge,
knowing that being able to feel anything at all was a blessing
i now know that i was anything but jaded before.
we all like to carry the pretense that we've transcended the
capacity for torment, but every utterance of that declaration
has been made in vain
weariness has an invisible weight
which makes each step heavier,
sorrow has a vice-like grip on your mind which can blind you,
but the worst affliction is the exhaustion;
an unwillingness to throw yourselves amongst the anger which
clouds the atmosphere
but still, through the smog, i kept walking in a direction which
made sense
his business card was still in my pocket,
i wondered if my path would take me back to him,
but it never did
i got on a bus out of New York
hopped on the first Greyhound bus to Washington using the
money he gave me for a phone
maybe i did it because deep down i knew where i had to go,
or maybe, i'd just seen too many films depicting the very same
beat authors had plenty to answer for
Kerouac's freedom was always an envy of mine
his sepia colored adventures
which allowed him to meander through America before we all
got distracted,
before we all got consumed by hate,
which now had so many faces

disconnected

i looked over the shoulder of the woman sat in front of me on
the bus as she frantically
scrolled looking for meaning on her phone, fumbling around for
a connection, only to find discordant hate
it's funny,
that social media still goes by the same name
given the contempt which bitter minds congregate around,
toying with new ways to attempt to be profound
but what if they don't want their wit to be applauded, what if
they just want to be seen?
what if they just want a solid foothold on the ladder which we all
must climb to find our way in the world,
the more worlds you tear apart,
the more truths you decimate
the higher you stand
pitchforks and persecution are now digitalized
pick your virtue,
repeat it until the foam on your lips taste of it
project your vitriolic disgust
until you're encompassed by self-righteous morality
pretend your body will putrefy with superiority
after subverting yourself into the delusion
we can ever truly be free of imperfection

construct yourself as purity personified
put the lacerations on your own back,
as you pretend you're the chastised
after you've chosen your target,
any adversary will suffice;
they'll take the fall for your ego's fragility
as though they were the ones to blame,
that you seek out all of the hate in the world
that your inadequacy shines through the spite,
as though you've lived your life better
transfixed by hate

grasp subjective disgust
until your pulse knows to quicken
you'll remember every word you said once your body fails

which words do you want to accompany you in the dark?

the eve of war

the first words i read after my return
were scrawled on the walls of my school;
anarchist graffiti in the place where memorial flowers were once
laid out for me
the spray paint demanded the reader to eat the rich,
it was the first time that it truly dawned on me,
that their hunger was not only felt in their despair,
but also in their hollow stomachs
"nothing in life is free" so they say,
but we weren't created cash in hand,
it seems, that's been forgotten along the way
everyone has to pay their dues,
debt is a lottery for each new child born

the school was empty, half-boarded up,
parents had started to refuse to send their children there for the
last decade,
i wasn't the last to die in the hallways,
the classrooms, the courtyard outside,
even blood had been shed in the bathrooms -
as girls applied their lip gloss and combed their hair frustrated
boys locked onto their targets
all they wanted was to be between their legs
without having to treat them with a shred of respect

how could the world be so cruel to them?

how many lives had the locked gates saved?
how many more simply died on the streets instead, without ever
having to learn trigonometry or biology?

i suppose it's no use to any of us now
our intellect is ultimately a hindrance,
it permitted us to see the true odious nature
of those born into the privilege
of handing out oppression,
force-feeding degradation into
the mouths that cried for progress
but true actualization teaches us, that we cast the villains,
there are always going to be those willing to play those roles
no amount of insight could change the world now
too many buttons had been pushed
the war begun years ago,
our time was always running out
but still, houses were sold,
and overtime hours were clocked in,
people slammed the soles of their feet
onto treadmills and did their admin

only now had a new war been brought to America
in a way, the time felt right
we'd dropped so many bombs

yet known so little of the devastation
we could watch the fireworks on TV, but even then,
the macabre horror of war failed to resonate
it didn't matter how intellectual, academic,
or empathetic we were
no one could truly know how it feels to watch bodies of your
neighbors drop to the floor,
to see blood running into the gutters,
to catch the smell of death in your nostrils
the rest of the world gave us a warning,
the president didn't respond to threats well,
she rolled out the welcome mat for the carnage which would rain
down on all the ordinary people – she never cared for them
anyway

for years, the rich have been able to retreat to bunkers

filled with champagne and

socialite hooker to fuck while the rest of the world
deals with the fallout

ordinary people have just been side characters in the events
which shaped the world – contorting it beyond natural function
news anchors informed us that there was no question if the
bombs were coming or not

the question was, where would they land

was it finally time for the nuclear war we've anticipated ever
since there were big red buttons to press?

they say all good things must come to an end, but what about
the bad?

what about the constant fear, oppression, and hate?
will that end too, all by the grace of a nuclear explosion?

i shouldn't have hoped for it,
knowing that death is no reprieve,
just an endless expanse of unsated consciousness that has no
motivation,
because it has no capacity for action
but on the eve of war i smiled,
perhaps with the same appetite for destruction
which Metallica had drummed into me;
a tribal drum beat calling the apocalypse

an existentialist's offer to the world

i used to want to write for you,
make the agony fade,
make perspectives shift so they never have to be clouded by the
same ennui as mine
but now i'm not sure
i could bear to feel a pen in the hand, or the pressure
of the keys as my torment is transcribed for voyeuristic pleasure
there are no words of comfort left anyway,
words invite bombs,
they're not too effective at disinviting them
preachers and pundits may be well meaning, but the world has
come to distrust peace and sanctity,
finding assurance in the knowledge, that someone or something
is suffering for our success

in bloom

i've lost count of the time i've romanticized the vision
of mushroom clouds blossoming in the sky
erasing humanity
i imagined the bliss of the searing heat
hitting me with the affirmation that sufferance would end
not just for me,
but for the world itself,
we'd become too accustomed to greed
to want to fall away from the idea of the American dream
which was no longer on sale
happy families behind white picket fences
seemed an archaic illusion
now, lovers lie alienated in apartments choked on their sadness,
the picket fences are now picket lines -
bitterness lies at the core of what it is to be human
maybe the apocalypse and the rapture,
were always supposed to be one in the same
maybe we'd forgotten how to live freely,
so we malleably bent to sold ideals

a nihilist's dream

has anyone in history lived,
and not asked what happens in death?
has anyone in history lived,
and got to the finish line without regret?
are we any different from wounded animals,
trapped in the headlights of mortality,
frozen in fear awaiting what we've longed to understand
terrified of the final realization?
of course not,
our obsession with what divides us
has driven us away from narratives of what makes us the same
i used to be like you -
worse in fact,
my alienation devoured me,
my frustration
splintered any hopes i had
of putting my sorrow behind me,
it was a trend to be in agony,
so i grabbed compasses,
stuck the needles in my arm – scribing fashion,
a nihilist's declaration,
it didn't matter how deep the wounds went,
they were all just scratches on the surface
compared to the torturous carousel
which would twirl in my mind every night
if resurrection has taught me but one thing,
it's to grasp commonality when you can -
wrap both thighs around it,
make declarations of infatuation and never let go

my olive branch to humanity

sirens cut through the air,
traffic swelled through the city streets,
voices shrieked in panic;
we were in the eye of the man-made storm
this was exactly how i anticipated the end
mass hysteria feeding into a frantic scramble of fear
the radio forewarned that the Enemy's
artillery was only moments away,
but for the first time in my life,
i kept true to my name
i walked amongst the chaos,
as though i was kicking through fallen autumn leaves
yet, i didn't want to feel alone
i'd spent my entire life
putting myself in the line of fire of loneliness
closing the curtains,
bolting the door,
turning off my phone,
and still waiting for someone to come and save me
who was ever going to catch me if no one saw me fall?

if the end was truly coming, i had put myself in the way of the
greatest harm,
without truly knowing the reason,
but if death had taught me anything,
it taught me to trust my intuition and those mixed feelings that
churn inside of us and argue with our minds
i picked up the handset of a rusted payphone,
looking at all the adverts for company for the night,
whilst dialing the number
hoping to have some of my very own

he answered
i choked
as i introduced myself as the girl from the park,
knowing there was only moments
before the connection was cut
and i'd find myself amongst the noxious smog and dark

he seemed kinder,
when i couldn't see his face,
his chiseled aesthetic
which made my resurrected heart race
everyone needs a friend for the end of the world,
it just so happened mine was a stranger,
as alone as i,
in a penthouse suite,
sipping Bollinger champagne
snorting lines of cocaine
chopped by his American Express Centurion credit card
"you look like you could teach me a thing or two"
he drawled through wired lips,
"what would you like to know?"
i held comfort in knowing
in what may be his final moments he had a guide -
something i never had,
something no one ever has,
but i told him,

what awaits on the other side
"was it all for nothing then?"
"you'll have the rest of your existence to decide,
don't sour your final moments with lament"
"make a final memory,
don't numb yourself to reality"

i placed down the receiver,
with a heavy heart,
but a slither of relief
slipped through my mind
knowing that there could never be any other time
where a resurrected bipolar poet could comfort the rich
yet it's he who gave me a final lesson about the world
i'd come to relish in the warmth of my self-righteous beliefs that
anyone who hated me was repugnant –
as though i had it all figured out,
as though i had learned nothing
from coming back to life
that even the worst of us crave life
even a life filled with disasters and torture

warheads vs crowbars

if the figures were to be believed, 6000 nuclear warheads shared
the ground i walked on
most have been having nightmares
about a nuclear bombs since the Cold War
was this day always destined to come?
were the lives of
citizens always going to be ripped apart this way?
no more trips to the grocery store,
no more Netflix binges, eating ice cream out of the tub,
no more birthdays celebrated,
no more moments of elation and fear as you tell someone that
you love someone for the first time
no more anxiety,
no more lust,
no more heartbreak

just silence and dust

all due to a pissing contest between
two leaders who never knew the meaning of leadership
if only crowbars had been placed in their hands instead
but there's no honor in fighting to the death anymore,
if thousands of lives aren't the price paid for victory

it's categorized as violence

sound of drums

from the moment the first warhead was born,
the chance of it being detonated was there -
a lingering possibility,
another prospect of another
apocalyptic disaster to mentally contend with,
along with climate change or another new plague

the sands of time slipped
until there was justification,
to detonate again
Hiroshima invited a darkened sky;
smoke and fire crackling
through the architecture
140,000 deaths wasn't enough to lay to rest our atomic arsenal

instead, it grew larger,

capable of mutually assured destruction – what use was the
planet if humanity couldn't reap the profits
but don't think of us as victims –
not with our promise of a counterstrike
sure, it wasn't every American with their hand on the trigger,

but we were all equally as responsible
every ripple of hate and greed fed into the atmosphere

and led us to this point
a post-truth humanity,
where only the rich are believed, and the poor are parrots to be
deceived
it takes one person to stand up and be the change;
Pope Francis and the Dalai Lama were right, all this time
yet neither sold us an ideal worth investing in

our mortal lives may just be a blip in the cosmos,
and our footprints may fade away in time, but we leave behind
echoes of our intent,

wisps of consciousness
which feed into the atmosphere
it goes beyond the nature vs nurture debate
we're the ones who shape the earth
think of it as a video game,
where most of the time you're in control,
but for the most part,
your programmed path guides you,
the one choice which is truly ours, is the choice between right
and wrong

dooms day clock

it's been two minutes to midnight
for as long as i can remember

generations have lived and
died waiting for the hands to strike twelve
paralysed by the prospect of the apocalypse,
has it always been just a matter of time?
or has our ego tricked us into believing
that we'll be the ones to see the end?
life on earth has breathed for 3.5 billion years,
but how many anxious breaths have been drawn in, awaiting the
inevitable end
i never did like the prospect of dying alone,
i thought of it as leaving a party early,
and leaving behind joy, sex, narcotics, music, and euphoria
but now i can see,
that me and the world are intrinsically combined
we exist in each other,
whether i'm dead or alive
with fear evading me,
i could see clearly,
it was just another false alarm
i turned a smile as i recounted TS Elliot's infamous words -

"this is the way the world ends, not with a bang but a whimper"
It's the End of the World as We Know It, and I Feel Fine

crowds outside of Washington gathered as the sky turned to a
muddy black
radio waves silent,
TV studios abandoned,
social media blocked
some held signs,
some held candles,
some held the ones they loved in their arms
i held the knowledge,
that this was just another lesson in fear

the ice caps are melting,
terrorists are hoarding bombs,
the planet is getting warmer,
forest fires blaze,
but no one is masochistic enough to invite a counterstrike
i left them amongst the comfort of their catastrophe,
wading into the widespread panic reminded of wild animals
snared in the teeth of a predator above them in the food chain
death is no picnic,
but neither is living,
if i was going to fall for the fear, they would have had to
confront me with true horror

the people in charge always have an air around them –
which tells you that they know more
but they're just afraid as us
in their $5000 suits, driving their Tesla cars,
and checking their Rolexes

if you're looking for authority, look to nature

apocalypse vs reality

reality isn't in the habit of matching expectation

what makes you believe it would
be different with the end of the world?

whether you're waiting for catastrophe of that lightning bolt of
ardent passion hitting as you fall in love, nothing ever truly
works out how we imagined

we should have taken this as a sign that there are greater forces
at work than our own minds,
but we're too stubborn for that
too blind in the belief that just because we can see the forest and
the trees, we have a grasp on reality

a final resurging note

if i came back for anything,
i came to tell you to wake up while you're still alive

love remains, when all else has faded to dust

let your faith evolve and forget the notion
of the cozy catastrophe where you're swept away from
responsibility and expectations

don't go in search of the Kool-Aid to drink –

life is just a ride with no safety guarantee, our mortality is a gift
which we shouldn't be so keen to return to the sender

we've allowed 1984 to become a self-fulfilling prophecy –

a welcome dystopia which celebrated our fears

let the post-apocalyptic fiction gather dust and

look to the poets for inspiration

through their misery and adversity, their passion never faded –

they found the words to pull beauty from
the most unlikely of crevices

Amelia Vandergast is the author of *Whispers In The Gallery: An Anthology of Smoking Pains*.

Follow Amelia Vandergast on Twitter:

@AmeliaVPoetry

Joseph Leo Hickey lives in Virginia. He is the author of eight other poetry books, including *Baptism of Apathy*, *Unity*, *Love Poems at The End of Our Lives*, *Liefie*, *The Last Poem*, *Purity: Redeemed*, *The Penultimate Poems* and *Harmonie*. He is currently 27 years old.

His upcoming books are *I Know Nothing but Miracles*, and *Baptism of Apathy* (Volumes 2-14).

YouTube: allthestarsaredead

joseph@melodiumhouse.com